T0034977

GEO~GRAPHICS
Regina Giménez

This is an Em Querido book
Published by Levine Querido

LEVINE QUERIDO

www.levinequerido.com • info@levinequerido.com
Levine Querido is distributed by Chronicle Books LLC
Text copyright © 2021 by Zahori Books
Illustrations © 2021 by Regina Giménez
Translator © 2022 by Alexis Romay and Valerie Block
Originally published in Catalan by Zahori Books
All rights reserved
Library of Congress Control Number: 2021943715
ISBN 978-1-64614-130-2
Printed and bound in China

Published May 2022
First printing

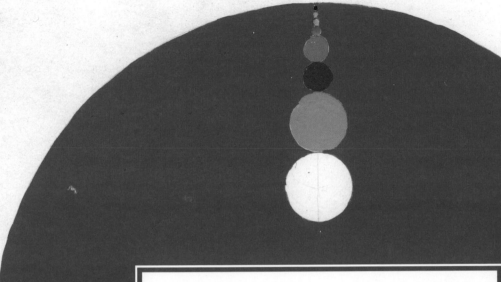

GEO~GRAPHICS
Regina Giménez

Translated by
Alexis Romay and Valerie Block

LQ

LEVINE QUERIDO
MONTCLAIR · AMSTERDAM · HOBOKEN

Table of Contents

The universe is enormous — and it's brimming with secrets and surprising curiosities.

You may have asked yourself: Why does the Sun in the sky look different from other planets and stars in our galaxy? Why doesn't the Moon appear at the same time as the Sun? How did lakes and deserts and mountains form on Earth? What makes rivers flow the way they do?

In this book you will find answers to these questions in a fun and magical way — through shapes and colors. Planets and stars, continents and islands, rivers and lakes, volcanoes and hurricanes . . . here they are transformed into circles, polygons, lines, and spirals that help to explain the world around us. In this unusual atlas of the universe's many wonders, science and art meet like never before.

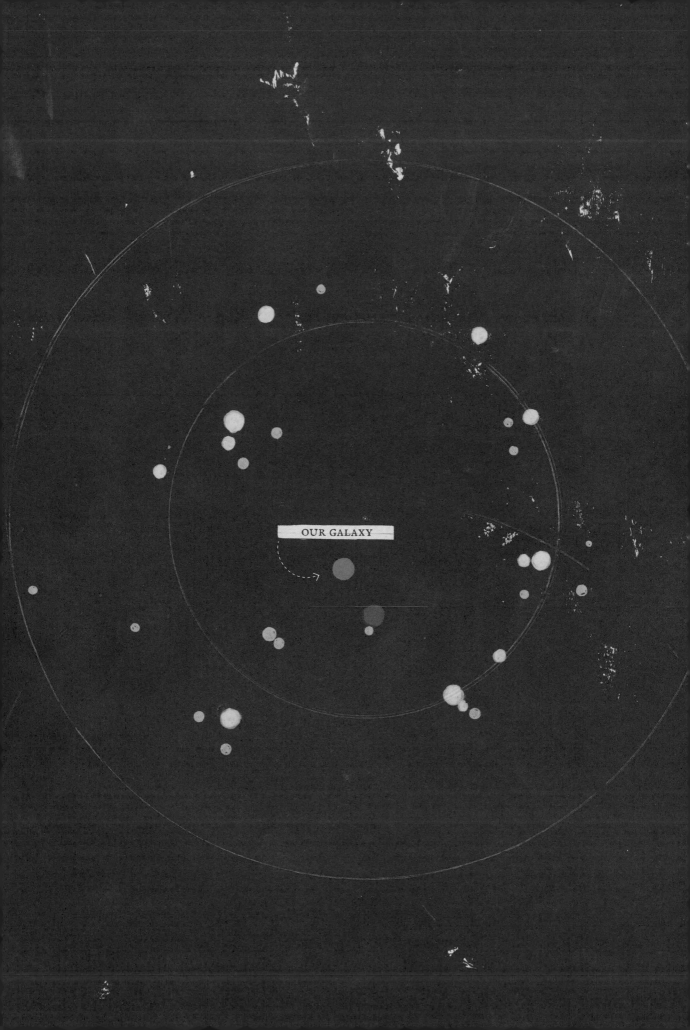

OUR GALAXY

Chapter I

THE UNIVERSE

The universe is everything that exists: the planets, the stars, the gigantic clouds of dust and gas — and the enormous space between them all.

Nobody knows how big the universe is, or even if it is the only one that exists.

Distances between things in the universe are enormous, and special units are used to measure them, such as light years.

Within this immense space, we live on a miniscule dot: our home planet, Earth.

Earth is one of the eight planets that orbit (or revolve around) our Sun, which is a star. Like all stars, the Sun emits its own light. By contrast, planets and satellites (or moons) do not have light — they reflect the light of the stars.

If objects in the universe are near one another, they will attract each other with the force of gravity. That is why some of them orbit. Together, the planets and Sun comprise our solar system.

The *BIG* BANG

About 13.8 billion years ago, the universe was very different from what it is now.

All of existence was concentrated into a single, dense, and extremely hot point. That single point began to expand in a manner similar to a big explosion, an event we now call the Big Bang.

This is the origin of matter. In the expansion, particles began to cool; then they came together to form the very first stars. In time, these stars began to group together, forming galaxies. As some galaxies collided with others, the universe became populated with new stars, as well as asteroids, comets, and planets.

The universe continues to expand, and nobody knows if it will ever stop.

IRREGULAR GALAXY

SPIRAL GALAXY

ELLIPTICAL GALAXY

The GALAXIES

In the universe, there are at least 200
billion galaxies — immense gatherings
of dust, gas, and stars.

They give shelter to whole planetary systems, and may take
on different shapes — spiral, elliptical, or irregular forms.
Galaxies tend to revolve around their own centers. They move
through space and sometimes even collide with each other!

The galaxy in which we live is
called the Milky Way.

It is called the Milky Way because from Earth, at night,
we can see a strip as white as milk crossing the sky like a
road. It has the shape of a spiral with four "arms," and
our solar system is located in one of those arms.

The COLOR of the STARS

When we look at the sky at night, we see a multitude of stars shining in the darkness. On first sight they might seem to look the same — but if we observe them closely, or look at them through a telescope, we realize that they have distinct colors: blue, white, yellow, orange, red . . .

The stars are giant balls of gas
that generate light and heat.

Their light shines as different colors, depending
on the amount of heat they emit.

The hottest stars are blue and
can reach up to nearly 90,000 degrees Fahrenheit.

The next-hottest are the blue-white stars, then the white ones, the yellow-white ones, the yellow ones, the orange ones, and, finally, the red ones, which are the coldest. The color of a star gives us clues about its age, because, like humans, stars are born and then eventually die. When they are young, they emit a lot of energy and burn at a higher temperature.

As time passes,
stars lose heat, until
finally, they fade.

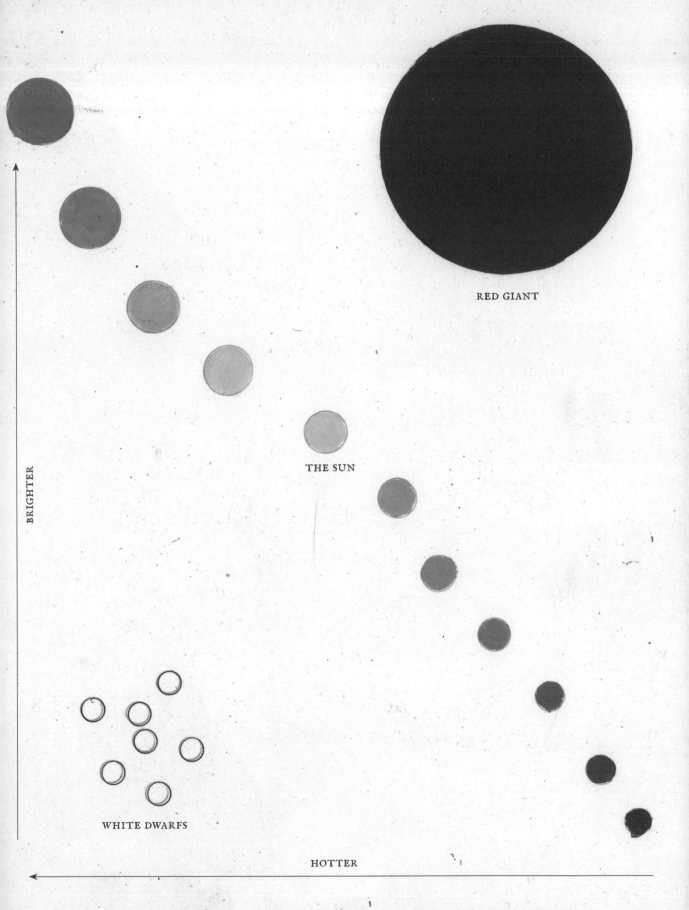

RED GIANT

BRIGHTER

THE SUN

WHITE DWARFS

HOTTER

THE RELATIONSHIP BETWEEN COLOR AND TEMPERATURE

SUN

MERCURY

VENUS

EARTH

MARS

JUPITER

SATURN

URANUS

NEPTUNE

The ORBIT of the PLANETS

The solar system has existed for some 4.5 billion years. It has a star — the Sun — and eight planets that orbit it.

The four that revolve nearest to the Sun (Mercury, Venus, Earth, and Mars) are solid masses, and the planets farther away are mainly made of gas. Saturn is surrounded by a ring made up of ice and rocks, and it has more than 80 satellites orbiting it. Earth, by contrast, has only one moon.

In the solar system, there are many other objects revolving around the Sun. Beyond Neptune there are dwarf planets, like Pluto, which are smaller than the eight principal planets.

There are more than a million asteroids orbiting the Sun as well, along with smaller comets that leave a luminous wake when they pass near the Sun.

The DIAMETER of the PLANETS

The biggest of the planets in our solar system is,
by far, Jupiter, which is almost 11 times larger than Earth.
Even so, it is very small if we compare it to the Sun.

The Sun is so large, more than a million
planets like Earth could fit inside!

However, though it might seem enormous compared
to the planets that revolve around it, the Sun is still a
relatively average-sized star in our galaxy.

Earth is the fifth largest planet in the
solar system. It measures nearly 8,000
miles in diameter and is the biggest of
the four solid-mass planets.

Mercury is roughly one-third the size
of Earth, making it the smallest planet,
barely larger than our Moon.

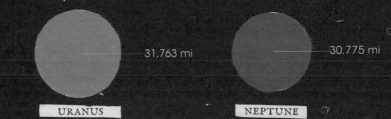

31,763 mi — URANUS

30,775 mi — NEPTUNE

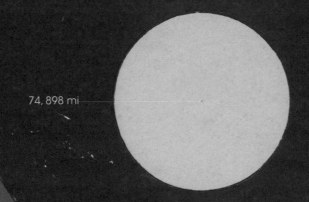

74,898 mi — SATURN

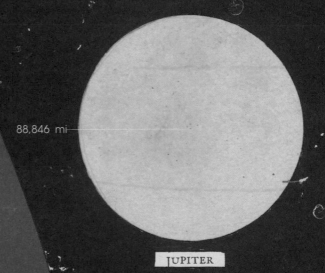

88,846 mi — JUPITER

SUN
864,337 mi

4,220 mi — MARS

7,926 mi — EARTH

7,521 mi — VENUS

3,032 mi — MERCURY

FROM MARS

FROM EARTH

FROM FERONIA*

FROM VENUS

FROM MAXIMILIANA*

FROM JUPITER

FROM SATURN

FROM URANUS

FROM NEPTUNE

FROM MERCURY

The **SUN** *as* **SEEN** *from the* **PLANETS**

The Sun is a star like the others we
can observe in the night sky. But it
seems much larger to us because
it is closer to our planet.

If instead of Earth we lived on Neptune, a planet in our
solar system much farther away from this star, the Sun
would barely be a shining dot in space. On the other hand,
from the planet closest to the Sun — Mercury — this star
would look three times bigger than what we see from
Earth, and its light seven times brighter.

* Feronia and Maximiliana are asteroids.

ECLIPSES

Earth turns around the Sun and at the same time, its satellite, the Moon, turns around Earth.

TOTAL ECLIPSE OF THE MOON

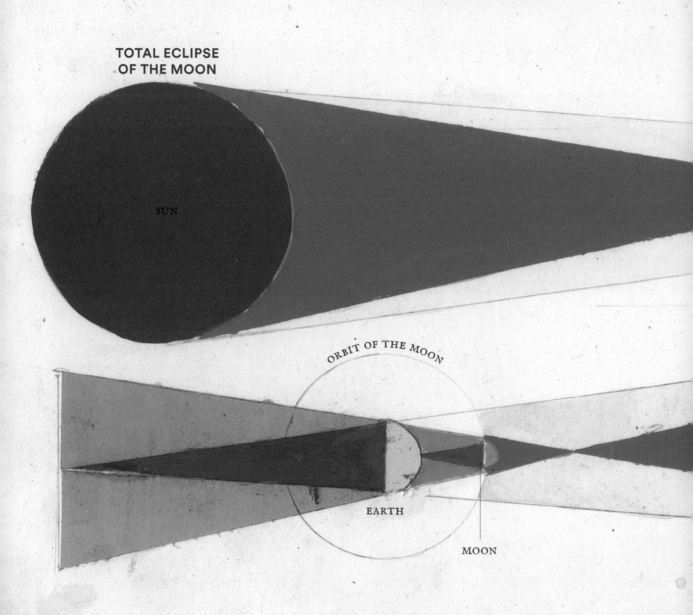

SUN

ORBIT OF THE MOON

EARTH

MOON

A lunar eclipse occurs when Earth finds
itself between the Sun and the Moon.

In this case, our planet projects its shadow onto
the Moon, which, little by little, is covered until it
is completely obscured by our planet.

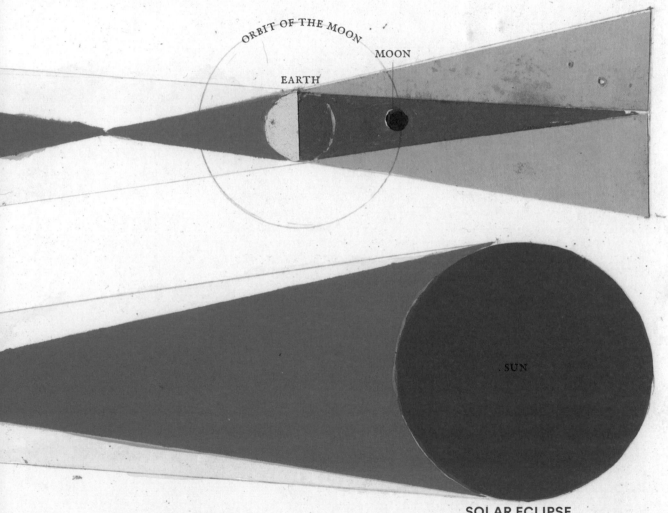

ORBIT OF THE MOON

MOON

EARTH

SUN

SOLAR ECLIPSE

When the Moon is situated between Earth and
the Sun, it projects its shadow over our planet,
and this causes a solar eclipse.

The effect is spectacular — it almost looks as if the Sun has
disappeared from the sky in broad daylight. But this eclipse
can only be seen from certain points on Earth.

The LUNAR PHASES

The Moon is a satellite of Earth, and like the planets, does not emit its own light. What we see when we look at the Moon is the light of the Sun reflected on its surface.

As the Moon orbits Earth, the Sun's rays don't always reach it in the same way. Therefore, we see the Moon as different shapes in the sky.

If light from the Sun fully hits the face of the Moon that is visible from Earth, we see a full Moon. But most of the time, depending on the Moon's position around Earth, we can only see a part of its surface.

The shapes of the Moon during its various phases are: new moon (we cannot see it) waxing moon (growing larger), full moon (complete) and waning moon (shrinking).

The different phases are repeated approximately once a month.

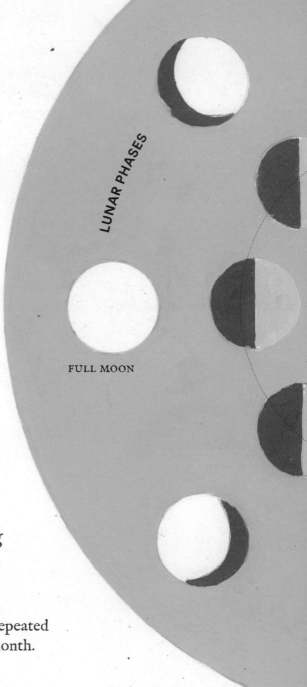

LUNAR PHASES

FULL MOON

WAXING
MOON

NEW MOON

SUNLIGHT

EARTH

WANING
MOON

Chapter II
THE EARTH

Ours is the only planet known to be inhabited by living beings. This life is possible because Earth has very special characteristics. For example, it is located close enough to the Sun to receive its light and heat, while also being surrounded by the atmosphere, a layer of gases that protect it from the most dangerous of solar rays. These gases help Earth retain heat and contain the oxygen we need to breathe.

Much of Earth's surface is covered by liquid water, which is essential to life.

Only a small part of Earth's surface emerges above water, in the form of continents and islands. The solid and rocky surface of Earth is called the crust. It is only a few miles deep in some parts, and although we are not aware of it, it is constantly moving. The crust is composed of various tectonic plates that fit together like a jigsaw puzzle and shift slowly over the mantle, which is a layer mostly composed of molten rock that flows below the crust. When the edges of these plates slide against each other, they cause earthquakes — they make us remember that under our feet, Earth's plates are always moving!

The very top of the mantle, just below the crust, is solid rather than molten. Together, the crust and the uppermost part the mantle are called the lithosphere.

EXOSPHERE:
BEGINNING AT 311 mi
FROM EARTH

THERMOSPHERE: 53-311 mi

MESOSPHERE: 31-53 mi

STRATOSPHERE: 6-31 mi

TROPOSPHERE: 0-6 mi

EARTH

The *The* ATMOSPHERIC LAYERS

The atmosphere is composed of various layers that surround Earth like a protective shield. The closest layer to the Earth's surface is the troposphere — this is the air that we breathe, and the clouds in the sky.

In the troposphere, rain, lightning, and winds are produced. The next layer above that is the stratosphere, which contains ozone, a gas that protects us from ultraviolet rays from the Sun. These types of rays are dangerous to our health.

Next, the mesosphere shields us from meteors. Meteors travel easily through space and the exosphere, but once they reach the mesosphere, gases in the air cause them to burn up. The International Space Station, which revolves around Earth, is located in the next layer, the thermosphere. And farther on, at 311 miles away, begins the exosphere, which separates us from deep space. The exosphere is an enormous zone that is very cold and contains vast amounts of space — there is no breathable air in this zone. Weather satellites (created by meteorologists to monitor weather patterns) orbit Earth in the exosphere, at around 22,300 miles.

The EARTH'S LAYERS

Earth is made mainly of rock. In the surface layer,
or lithosphere, these rocks are solid.

But as we go deeper into the interior, the
temperature gets hotter and hotter, until
the rocks start to break apart and fuse into
a viscous mass, similar to caramel.

This is the mantle, a layer of Earth about 1,802
miles thick. Even farther inside is the planet's
core, composed almost entirely of the metals iron
and nickel. On the outer core, these metals are
liquid — they are melted by the heat.

However, at the heart of the planet,
pressure is so high that the metals
become totally concentrated — they
form a solid, spherical inner core.

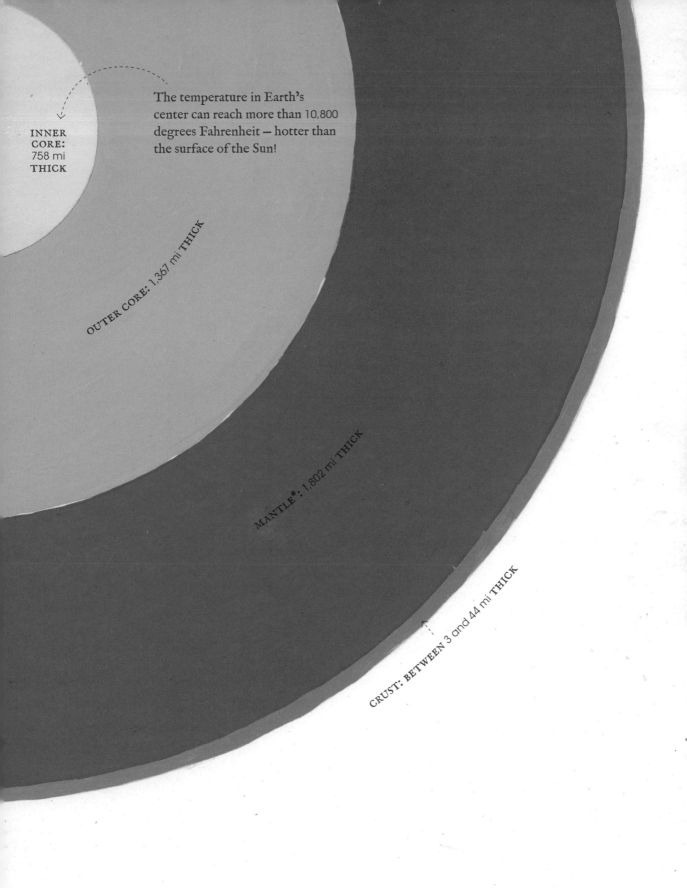

INNER
CORE:
758 mi
THICK

The temperature in Earth's
center can reach more than 10,800
degrees Fahrenheit — hotter than
the surface of the Sun!

OUTER CORE: 1,367 mi THICK

MANTLE*: 1,802 mi THICK

CRUST: BETWEEN 3 and 44 mi THICK

* The mantle includes the upper mantle, a smaller transition
zone, and then the lower mantle.

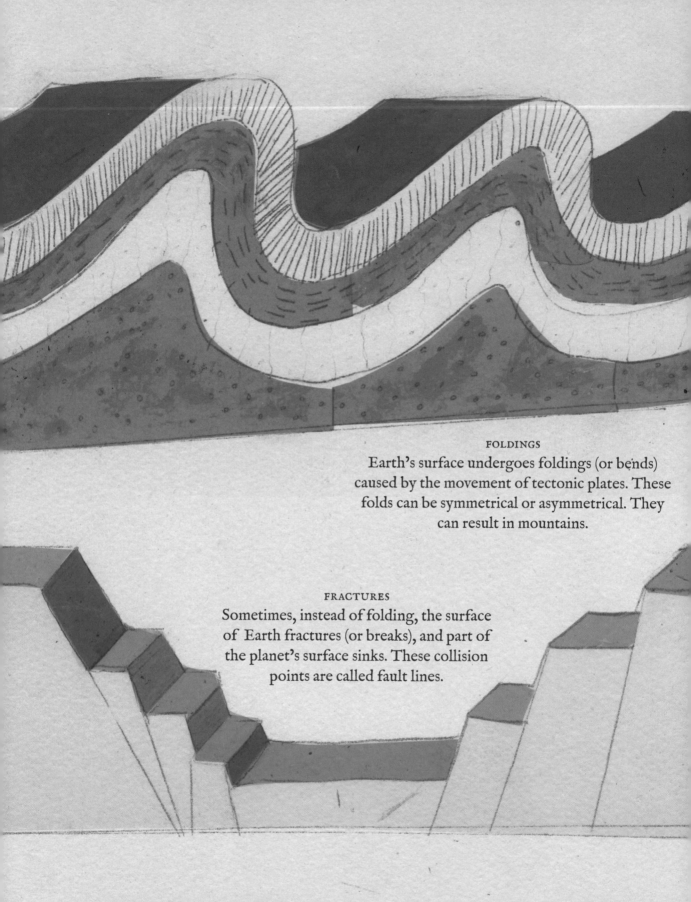

FOLDINGS

Earth's surface undergoes foldings (or bends) caused by the movement of tectonic plates. These folds can be symmetrical or asymmetrical. They can result in mountains.

FRACTURES

Sometimes, instead of folding, the surface of Earth fractures (or breaks), and part of the planet's surface sinks. These collision points are called fault lines.

TECTONIC PLATES

Sometimes the tectonic plates on Earth's
surface collide against each other and
bend, producing folded rock on the crust.

At other times, the plates separate, creating cracks through
which magma (or molten rock) escapes. The plates also can
slide under each other, producing a fracture between two
masses — which creates what is known as a fault.

These changes in the crust create mountains,
valleys, and trenches all over the world. In
the regions where the edges of tectonic
plates meet, these collisions, faults, and folds
produce volcanoes and earthquakes.

MAGNITUDE *of* EARTHQUAKES

Earthquakes are tremors caused by the movement of Earth's tectonic plates.

When these plates slide against one another, an enormous amount of energy is unleashed, creating seismic waves that make Earth's surface tremble and shake.

The point at which the earthquake originates, in the interior of the crust, is called the hypocenter. The point of the surface just above where it originates is called the epicenter. The earthquake's greatest intensity is felt at this epicenter.

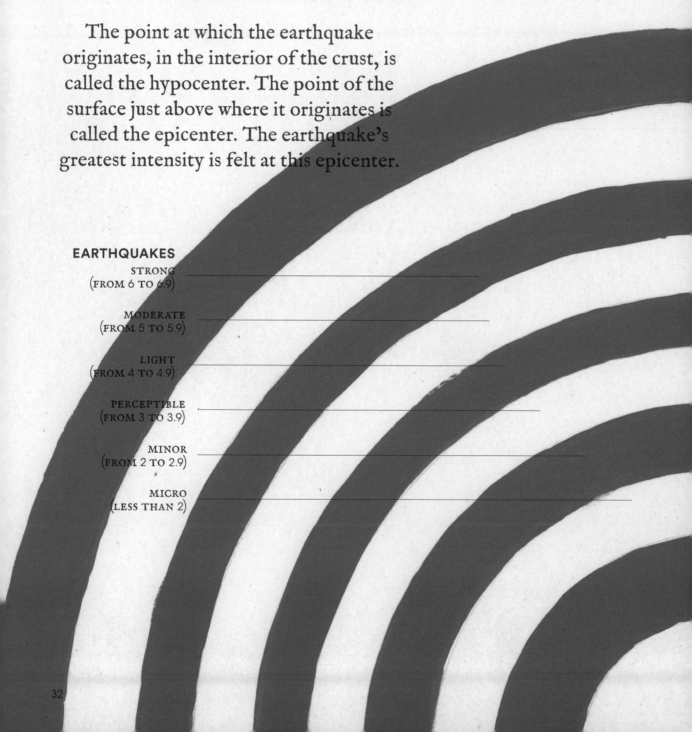

EARTHQUAKES

STRONG
(FROM 6 TO 6.9)

MODERATE
(FROM 5 TO 5.9)

LIGHT
(FROM 4 TO 4.9)

PERCEPTIBLE
(FROM 3 TO 3.9)

MINOR
(FROM 2 TO 2.9)

MICRO
(LESS THAN 2)

The Moment Magnitude Scale is used to measure earthquakes, classifying them by their intensity from 0 to 8 and above. For example, an earthquake of a magnitude between 2 and 3 on this scale releases energy similar to that of a moderate lightning bolt.

If an earthquake is between 6 and 7, its force is comparable to an atomic bomb.

EARTHQUAKES

GREAT
(FROM 8 TO LARGER)

MAJOR
(FROM 7 TO 7.9)

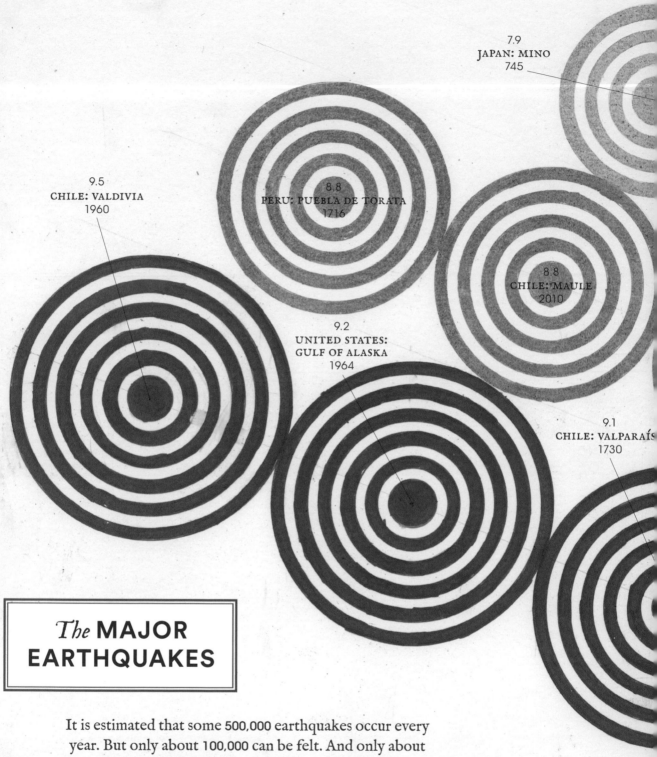

7.9
JAPAN: MINO
745

9.5
CHILE: VALDIVIA
1960

8.8
PERU: PUEBLA DE TORATA
1716

8.8
CHILE: MAULE
2010

9.2
UNITED STATES:
GULF OF ALASKA
1964

9.1
CHILE: VALPARAÍS
1730

The MAJOR EARTHQUAKES

It is estimated that some 500,000 earthquakes occur every year. But only about 100,000 can be felt. And only about 100 of them are intense enough to cause damage.

The greatest earthquake registered up to now was in Valdivia, Chile, in 1960.

It scored a 9.5 on the Moment Magnitude Scale. But the deadliest earthquake ever recorded occurred in Shaanxi, China, in 1556: it reached a magnitude of 8.0, and caused about 830,000 deaths.

7.0
GREECE: ZAKYNTHOS
ISLAND
1633

7.0
JAPAN: BEPPU BAY
1596

6.8
TURKEY: ISTANBUL
1231

7.9
JAPAN: TOKAIDO
818

7.9
IRAN: QUMIS
856

7.9
PERU:
HUAYNAPUTINA VOLCANO
1600

8.7
PHILIPPINES:
MINDANAO ISLAND
1897

8.5
CHILE: ATACAMA
1922

8.0
COAST OF PERU
1513

9.1
INDONESIA: SUMATRA
2004

9.1
JAPAN: COAST OF HONSHU
2011

The SIZE of the CONTINENTS

The continents are large masses of land
that project above sea level.

Although today we can identify seven continents, there was a time
when they were all united in a single mass called Pangea. About
200 million years ago, because of movement in Earth's crust, this
supercontinent divided into several pieces, which began to move
away from each other and formed the current continents.

The largest continent is Asia, which
represents almost a third of the emerged land
formations on the planet.

North and South America together make up nearly
another third of Earth's total land mass. The smallest
continent of all is Australia.

ASIA 17,212,000mi²

AFRICA 11,508,000 mi²

NORTH AMERICA 9,365,000mi²

SOUTH AMERICA 6,880,000 mi²

ANTARCTICA 5,400,000 mi²

EUROPE 3,837,000 mi²

AUSTRALIA/
OCEANIA
2,968,000 mi²

CONTINENTS *by* POPULATION

Our planet is inhabited by almost 7.8 billion people, and more than 60% of them live in Asia. The most populous countries — China and India — are both in Asia, and they each have more than 1 billion people.

The largest territories are not always the ones that have the largest number of inhabitants.

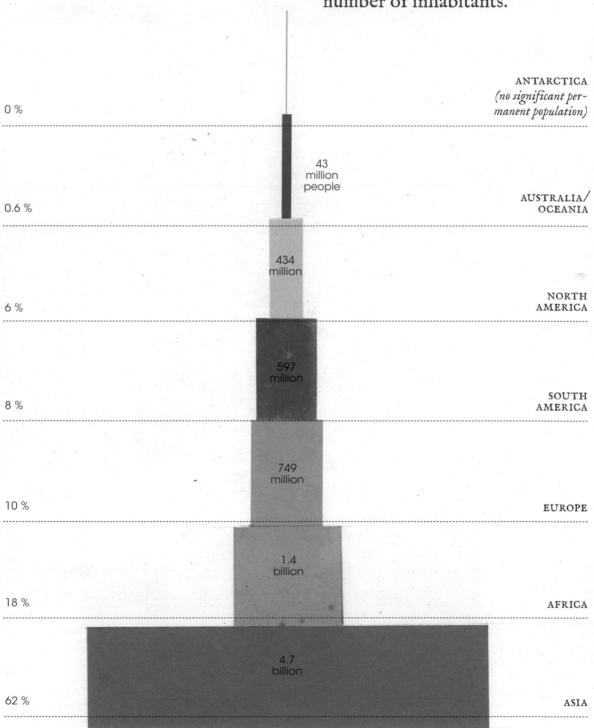

0 % — ANTARCTICA *(no significant permanent population)*

43 million people

0.6 % — AUSTRALIA/ OCEANIA

434 million

6 % — NORTH AMERICA

597 million

8 % — SOUTH AMERICA

749 million

10 % — EUROPE

1.4 billion

18 % — AFRICA

4.7 billion

62 % — ASIA

CONTINENTS
by **SURFACE AREA**

More people live in Europe than in North America, or South America, despite it being a much smaller continent by surface area.

Only 1,000-4,000 people live in Antarctica, which is larger than Europe, and these people only live there during a few seasons of the year.

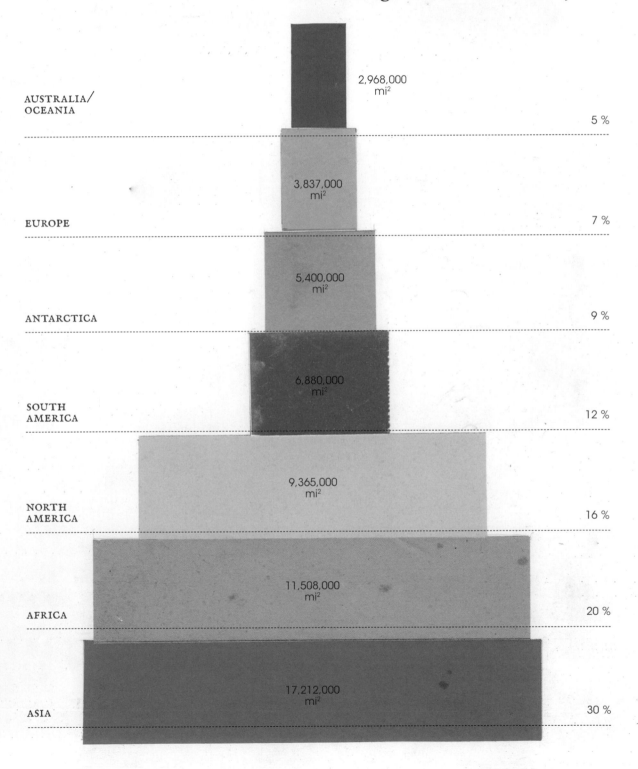

AUSTRALIA/
OCEANIA

2,968,000 mi²

5 %

EUROPE

3,837,000 mi²

7 %

ANTARCTICA

5,400,000 mi²

9 %

SOUTH AMERICA

6,880,000 mi²

12 %

NORTH AMERICA

9,365,000 mi²

16 %

AFRICA

11,508,000 mi²

20 %

ASIA

17,212,000 mi²

30 %

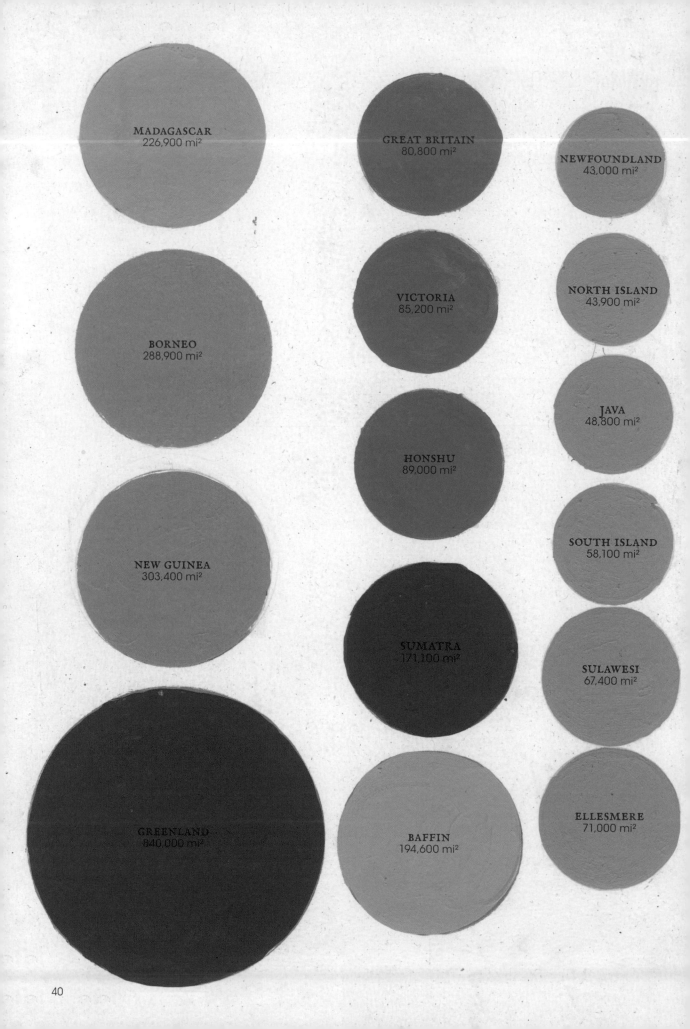

MADAGASCAR
226,900 mi²

GREAT BRITAIN
80,800 mi²

NEWFOUNDLAND
43,000 mi²

BORNEO
288,900 mi²

VICTORIA
85,200 mi²

NORTH ISLAND
43,900 mi²

HONSHU
89,000 mi²

JAVA
48,800 mi²

NEW GUINEA
303,400 mi²

SOUTH ISLAND
58,100 mi²

SUMATRA
171,100 mi²

SULAWESI
67,400 mi²

ELLESMERE
71,000 mi²

GREENLAND
840,000 mi²

BAFFIN
194,600 mi²

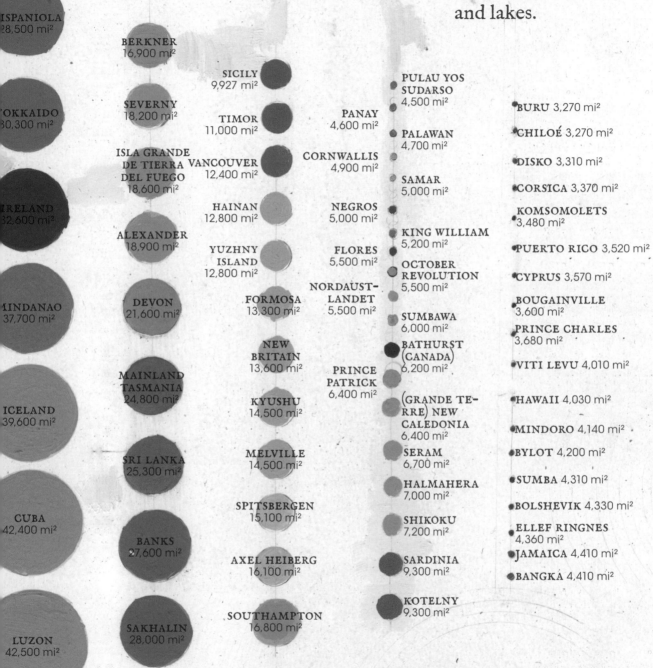

The 80 BIGGEST ISLANDS

There are thousands of islands spread out over the seas, oceans, and even in the middle of rivers and lakes.

ISPANIOLA 28,500 mi²

HOKKAIDO 30,300 mi²

IRELAND 32,600 mi²

MINDANAO 37,700 mi²

ICELAND 39,600 mi²

CUBA 42,400 mi²

LUZON 42,500 mi²

BERKNER 16,900 mi²

SEVERNY 18,200 mi²

ISLA GRANDE DE TIERRA DEL FUEGO 18,600 mi²

ALEXANDER 18,900 mi²

DEVON 21,600 mi²

MAINLAND TASMANIA 24,800 mi²

SRI LANKA 25,300 mi²

BANKS 27,600 mi²

SAKHALIN 28,000 mi²

SICILY 9,927 mi²

TIMOR 11,000 mi²

VANCOUVER 12,400 mi²

HAINAN 12,800 mi²

YUZHNY ISLAND 12,800 mi²

FORMOSA 13,300 mi²

NEW BRITAIN 13,600 mi²

KYUSHU 14,500 mi²

MELVILLE 14,500 mi²

SPITSBERGEN 15,100 mi²

AXEL HEIBERG 16,100 mi²

SOUTHAMPTON 16,800 mi²

PANAY 4,600 mi²

CORNWALLIS 4,900 mi²

NEGROS 5,000 mi²

FLORES 5,500 mi²

NORDAUST-LANDET 5,500 mi²

PRINCE PATRICK 6,400 mi²

PULAU YOS SUDARSO 4,500 mi²

PALAWAN 4,700 mi²

SAMAR 5,000 mi²

KING WILLIAM 5,200 mi²

OCTOBER REVOLUTION 5,500 mi²

SUMBAWA 6,000 mi²

BATHURST (CANADA) 6,200 mi²

(GRANDE TE-RRE) NEW CALEDONIA 6,400 mi²

SERAM 6,700 mi²

HALMAHERA 7,000 mi²

SHIKOKU 7,200 mi²

SARDINIA 9,300 mi²

KOTELNY 9,300 mi²

BURU 3,270 mi²

CHILOÉ 3,270 mi²

DISKO 3,310 mi²

CORSICA 3,370 mi²

KOMSOMOLETS 3,480 mi²

PUERTO RICO 3,520 mi²

CYPRUS 3,570 mi²

BOUGAINVILLE 3,600 mi²

PRINCE CHARLES 3,680 mi²

VITI LEVU 4,010 mi²

HAWAII 4,030 mi²

MINDORO 4,140 mi²

BYLOT 4,200 mi²

SUMBA 4,310 mi²

BOLSHEVIK 4,330 mi²

ELLEF RINGNES 4,360 mi²

JAMAICA 4,410 mi²

BANGKA 4,410 mi²

Some are truly tiny, with surface areas of less than one square mile.

Some islands are enormous, like Greenland. Others, like Great Britain or Honshu, have millions of inhabitants.

Chapter III

TOPOGRAPHY

The surface of our planet has transformed over time and it continues to change. Earth's crust is molded into different shapes and heights, both on firm ground and at the bottom of the oceans. On every continent there are plains, valleys, hills, and of course, mountains, that form the topography.

Many of the great mountain ranges that we know, like the Alps (Europe), the Himalayas (Asia), or the Andes (South America), were formed millions of years ago by collisions between tectonic plates, where one plate slides underneath another.

Some mountains are very tall and can reach a height of over **29,000** feet above Earth's average sea level.

Some mountains, or sometimes even entire islands, are the result of volcanic activity. Volcanoes originate in several ways: Sometimes, when two plates separate from one another, it creates a crack between which magma from Earth's mantle emerges. At other times, two plates crash into each other, causing high heat and pressure that forces magma to Earth's surface. There are also "hot spots" inside Earth that heat up magma and bring it to the surface.

Some volcanoes appear to be dormant (or asleep), but they can spew lava at any time!

MOUNTAIN PEAKS

The highest mountains in the world are found in Asia, where the Himalayan mountain range contains dozens of peaks higher than 22,000 feet above sea level. The Andes, in South America, is the longest mountain range in the world, with summits over 22,000 feet too, like Mount Aconcagua.

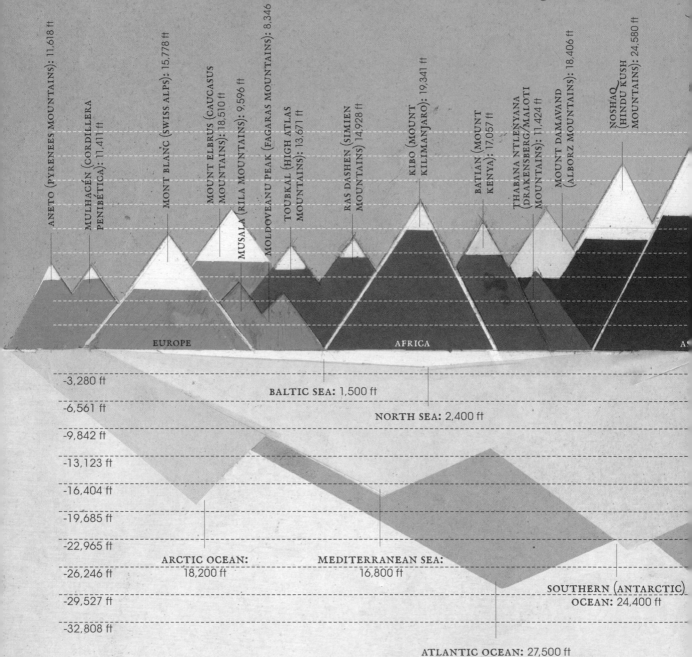

ANETO (PYRENEES MOUNTAINS): 11,618 ft

MULHACÉN (CORDILLERA PENIBÉTICA): 11,411 ft

MONT BLANC (SWISS ALPS): 15,778 ft

MOUNT ELBRUS (CAUCASUS MOUNTAINS): 18,510 ft

MUSALA (RILA MOUNTAINS): 9,596 ft

MOLDOVEANU PEAK (FAGARAS MOUNTAINS): 8,346 ft

TOUBKAL (HIGH ATLAS MOUNTAINS): 13,671 ft

RAS DASHEN (SIMIEN MOUNTAINS) 14,928 ft

KIBO (MOUNT KILIMANJARO): 19,341 ft

BATIAN (MOUNT KENYA): 17,057 ft

THABANA NTLENYANA (DRAKENSBERG/MALOTI MOUNTAINS): 11,424 ft

MOUNT DAMAVAND (ALBORZ MOUNTAINS): 18,406 ft

NOSHAQ (HINDU KUSH MOUNTAINS): 24,580 ft

EUROPE

AFRICA

A

-3,280 ft

BALTIC SEA: 1,500 ft

-6,561 ft

NORTH SEA: 2,400 ft

-9,842 ft

-13,123 ft

-16,404 ft

-19,685 ft

-22,965 ft

ARCTIC OCEAN: 18,200 ft

MEDITERRANEAN SEA: 16,800 ft

-26,246 ft

SOUTHERN (ANTARCTIC) OCEAN: 24,400 ft

-29,527 ft

-32,808 ft

ATLANTIC OCEAN: 27,500 ft

OCEAN DEPTHS

Beneath the seas and oceans, Earth's crust lies thousands of feet below the water's surface. Here, there are also mountains, volcanoes, and ocean trenches (deep, narrow chasms that sink thousands of feet into the crust).

In North America, the Rocky Mountains are the longest mountain range, extending about 3,000 miles from New Mexico in the United States all the way up to the northernmost part of British Columbia in Canada. In addition to these great mountain ranges around the world, there are very tall, ancient volcanoes on our planet that formed millions of years ago, like Mount Kilimanjaro in Africa — the tallest mountain that is not part of a mountain range.

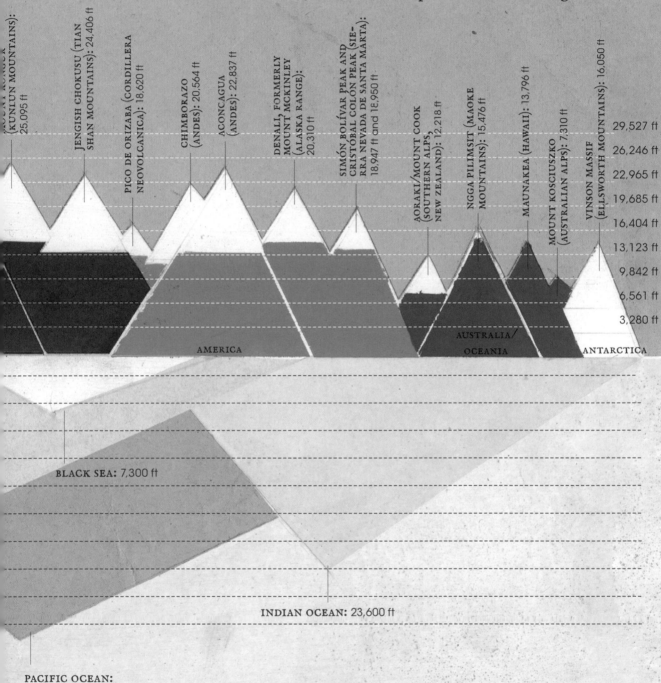

(KUNLUN MOUNTAINS): 25,095 ft

JENGISH CHOKUSU (TIAN SHAN MOUNTAINS): 24,406 ft

PICO DE ORIZABA (CORDILLERA NEOVOLCANICA): 18,620 ft

CHIMBORAZO (ANDES): 20,564 ft

ACONCAGUA (ANDES): 22,837 ft

DENALI, FORMERLY MOUNT MCKINLEY (ALASKA RANGE): 20,310 ft

SIMÓN BOLÍVAR PEAK AND CRISTÓBAL COLÓN PEAK (SIERRA NEVADA DE SANTA MARTA): 18,947 ft and 18,950 ft

AORAKI/MOUNT COOK (SOUTHERN ALPS, NEW ZEALAND): 12,218 ft

NGGA PILIMSIT (MAOKE MOUNTAINS): 15,476 ft

MAUNAKEA (HAWAII): 13,796 ft

MOUNT KOSCIUSZKO (AUSTRALIAN ALPS): 7,310 ft

VINSON MASSIF (ELLSWORTH MOUNTAINS): 16,050 ft

29,527 ft
26,246 ft
22,965 ft
19,685 ft
16,404 ft
13,123 ft
9,842 ft
6,561 ft
3,280 ft

AMERICA

AUSTRALIA/ OCEANIA

ANTARCTICA

BLACK SEA: 7,300 ft

INDIAN OCEAN: 23,600 ft

PACIFIC OCEAN: 36,000 ft

The deepest point on Earth is the Challenger Deep, some 35,000 feet below, found in the Pacific Ocean in the Mariana Trench. It is so deep that the Sun's light does not reach there, and it is inhabited by extraordinary animals like the Mariana snailfish and the sea pig.

The 14 «EIGHT-THOUSANDERS»

On Earth, only 14 peaks rise up more
than 26,247 feet (or 8,000 meters) —
the equivalent height of 25 Eiffel Towers
stacked on top of one another!

Known as the "Eight-Thousanders," these mountains are
located in the Himalayan and the Karakoram mountain
ranges, situated in Asia across China, Nepal, Bhutan, Pakistan,
Afghanistan, and India. At their summits, oxygen is so scarce
that human beings can survive only for about 20 hours.

Mount Everest, at 29,029 feet, has the honor
of being the highest point above average sea
level on the planet.

The Tibetan Plateau, which includes Mount
Everest and K2, is known as "the roof of the
world." After several failed attempts, in 1953
humans reached its summit for the first time.

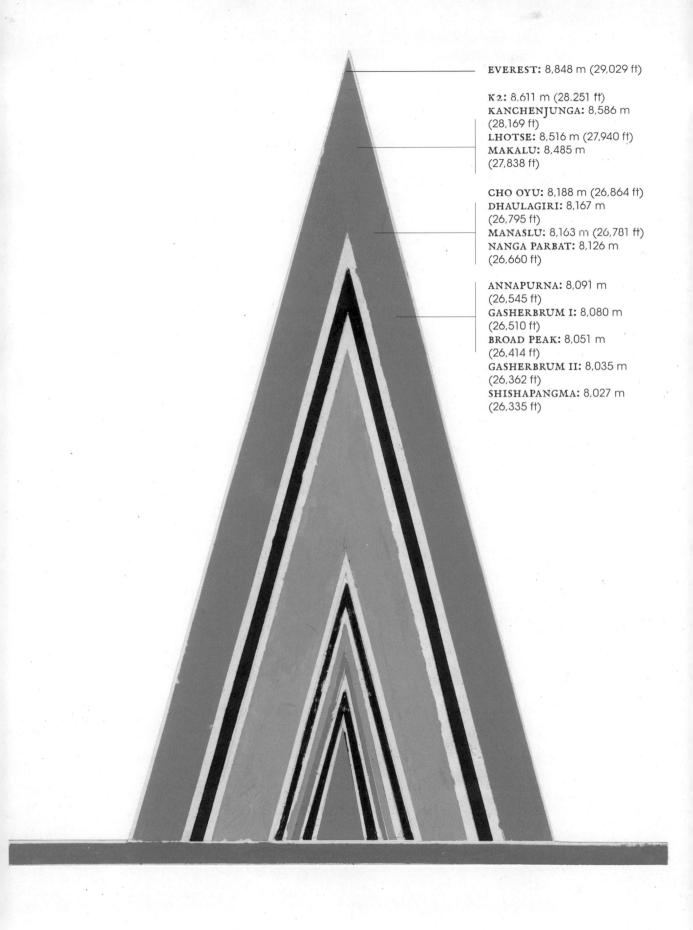

EVEREST: 8,848 m (29,029 ft)

K2: 8,611 m (28,251 ft)
KANCHENJUNGA: 8,586 m
(28,169 ft)
LHOTSE: 8,516 m (27,940 ft)
MAKALU: 8,485 m
(27,838 ft)

CHO OYU: 8,188 m (26,864 ft)
DHAULAGIRI: 8,167 m
(26,795 ft)
MANASLU: 8,163 m (26,781 ft)
NANGA PARBAT: 8,126 m
(26,660 ft)

ANNAPURNA: 8,091 m
(26,545 ft)
GASHERBRUM I: 8,080 m
(26,510 ft)
BROAD PEAK: 8,051 m
(26,414 ft)
GASHERBRUM II: 8,035 m
(26,362 ft)
SHISHAPANGMA: 8,027 m
(26,335 ft)

VOLCANOES

When a volcano begins to erupt,
magma from Earth's mantle gushes
up to the surface.

This magma comes up through a crevice called a conduit,
and emerges with great force through the upper part of
the volcano, called the crater (also known as the main
vent). Once the magma reaches the surface, it is called
lava. The lava flows in thick rivers down Earth's surface.

Volcanoes also send out gases, rocks,
and lots of ash, the latter of which
floats in the air and is transported
thousands of miles away.

THE MAIN TYPES OF VOLCANOES, BASED ON SHAPE

CINDER CONE

This is the simplest type of volcano, with a steep cone shape. Its lava is not fluid; it erupts pieces of solid lava (called cinder), along with ash and gases. The solid lava cools quickly, piling up around the crater. Cinder cones can reach up to **1,000** feet — not very tall compared to other volcano types.

COMPOSITE VOLCANO

Normally, these are very tall and have a conical form. Their magma is very viscous (or sticky), which means it traps gas within the volcano, allowing pressure to build up and eventually producing a strong explosion. This can create fissures on the sides of the principal conduit. Some of the tallest mountains are composite volcanoes, such as Ojos del Salado in Chile, which stands **22,615** feet above sea level.

SHIELD VOLCANO

These volcanoes have a characteristically wide base and low height. Shield volcanoes emit very fluid lava, which flows easily from the vent, rendering them less dangerous than volcanoes with viscous, explosive lava.

LAVA DOME

These volcanoes have very viscous lava that is too thick to flow away from the vent — instead, it solidifies and covers the crater, preventing gases from leaving. When these gases build up, the pressure can result in violent explosions. Lava domes often form within the craters of composite volcanoes.

ACTIVE VOLCANOES

 ERUPTION

 MINOR ACTIVITY OR ERUPTION ALERT

VOLCANIC DISTURBANCES

Most volcanoes can erupt at any moment. It is estimated there are 1500 active or potentially active volcanoes in the world. A volcano is considered extinct when it has been inactive for thousands of years.

 SEMISOPOCHNOI

GREAT SITKIN

SHISHALDIN

CLEVELAND

ALEUTIAN ISLANDS, ALASKA, AND NORTH AMERICA

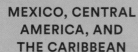 POPOCATÉPETL

TURRIALBA

SANTA MARÍA, SANTIAGUITO LAVADOME

 COLIMA

 FUEGO

 RINCÓN DE LA VIEJA

 PACAYA

 SOUFRIÈRE GUADALOUPE

 MASAYA

 KICK 'EM JENNY

 POÁS

MEXICO, CENTRAL AMERICA, AND THE CARIBBEAN

 NEVADOS DE CHILLÁN

 SANGAY

 SABANCAYA

 REVENTADOR

 NEVADO DEL RUIZ

 GALERAS

 CUMBAL

 CERRO NEGRO DE MAYASQUER

 VILLARRICA

 COPAHUE

PLANCHÓN-PETEROA

UBINAS

MACHÍN

 NEVADO DEL HUILA

SOUTH AMERICA

 YASUR

 ULAWUN

MAUNA LOA

LOPEVI

 MANAM

 AMBRYM

 KADOVAR

AOBA

 TINAKULA

   GAUA

PACIFIC OCEAN

EUROPE AND THE ATLANTIC OCEAN

 STROMBOLI

 ETNA

 CAMPI FLEGREI

AFRICA AND THE INDIAN OCEAN

 ERTA ALE

 NYIRAGONGO

 NYAMURAGIRA

 PITON DE LA FOURNAISE

 OI DOINYO LENGAI

 MAYOTTE

Most active volcanoes are part of the Ring of Fire in the Pacific Ocean.

ANTARCTICA

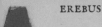 EREBUS

RING OF FIRE (FROM THE KURIL ISLANDS TO THE PHILIPPINES)

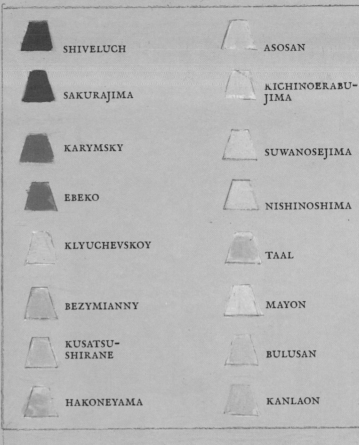

SHIVELUCH   ASOSAN

SAKURAJIMA   KICHINOERABU-JIMA

KARYMSKY   SUWANOSEJIMA

EBEKO   NISHINOSHIMA

KLYUCHEVSKOY   TAAL

BEZYMIANNY   MAYON

KUSATSU-SHIRANE   BULUSAN

HAKONEYAMA   KANLAON

INDONESIA

 DUKONO   KARANGETANG

 IBU   LOKON-EMPUNG

 SEMERU   SOPUTAN

 MERAPI   GAMALAMA

 SINABUNG   LEWOTOLOK

 AGUNG   BROMO

 SANGEANG API   BANDA API

 KRAKATAU   MARAPI

 KERINCI

Chapter IV

WATER

Earth is known as the Blue Planet. From space we can see this color because the oceans occupy much more surface area than the continents. Water is a fundamental part of our planet, as essential to us as it is for plants and animals.

For the most part, water on Earth is salty and can be found in the oceans and the seas. Only a small portion is fresh water.

This fresh water is found in lakes, rivers, and underground streams. There is also fresh water in frozen glaciers and in the ice found at the north and south poles, as well as in the atmosphere, where it exists as water vapor.

Water circulates throughout the entire planet.

Droplets from bodies of water and plant leaves evaporate because of the heat of the Sun. This water vapor ascends into the atmosphere, where it cools and condenses, forming clouds in the sky. The wind then moves these clouds, and the water falls in the form of rain, seeping into the ground or flowing into rivers — which are fed also by melting snow from the mountains. These rivers allow us to irrigate our plants and give us fresh water to drink. Rivers continue flowing into lakes, seas, or oceans, where the water cycle begins again.

The OCEANS

Water covers more than 70 % of the surface of the
planet. The continents are surrounded by an immense
mass of salt water, divided into five oceans.

The Pacific Ocean is the largest — it covers as much space as all the
continents put together, and it reaches from the coasts of North
and South America to Asia and Australia. The Atlantic Ocean, which
separates the Americas from Europe and Africa, is the second largest
and one of the most traveled. By size, the next largest is the Indian
Ocean, situated south of Asia, between Africa and Australia.

The oceans that surround the
poles are much smaller.

In the South the Antarctic Ocean surrounds the continent of
Antarctica. In the North, the Arctic Ocean is almost entirely covered
year-round by a layer of ice.

PACIFIC OCEAN: 62,500,000 mi²

ATLANTIC OCEAN: 32,900,000 mi²

INDIAN OCEAN: 27,200,000 mi²

SOUTHERN (ANTARCTIC) OCEAN: 8,500,000 mi²

ARCTIC OCEAN: 6,00,000 mi²

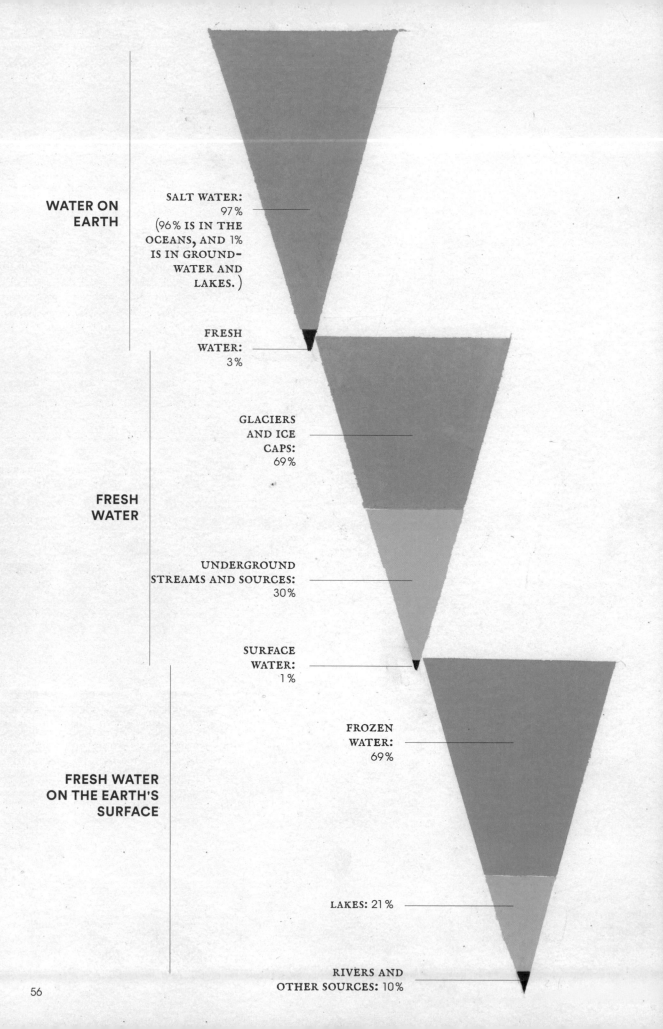

WATER ON
EARTH

SALT WATER:
97%
(96% IS IN THE
OCEANS, AND 1%
IS IN GROUND-
WATER AND
LAKES.)

FRESH
WATER:
3%

FRESH
WATER

GLACIERS
AND ICE
CAPS:
69%

UNDERGROUND
STREAMS AND SOURCES:
30%

SURFACE
WATER:
1%

FROZEN
WATER:
69%

FRESH WATER
ON THE EARTH'S
SURFACE

LAKES: 21%

RIVERS AND
OTHER SOURCES: 10%

The SOURCES *of* WATER

On Earth there are 332.5 million
cubic miles of water.

Only 2.5 % of our water is fresh water.
Most of it is found in the form of ice at
the poles, or glaciers — and the rest is
found underground. The fresh water
available in rivers and lakes makes up only
a tiny part of the total.

Lakes contain less than a hundredth
of the fresh water on Earth, and
rivers even less than that.

DRINKABLE WATER
In some parts of the planet, water is very scarce.
And sometimes, even when it is available, it's
not fit for human consumption because of
contamination. On Earth, one out of every
three people does not have access to safe
drinking water. This causes sickness, famine, the
extinction of other species, and even war.

The VOLUME of RIVERS

Though they make up only a tiny percentage of fresh water on Earth, rivers are the primary source of fresh water readily available to humans.

Because of this, the first human communities were established alongside rivers, and the great civilizations of the past flourished around their waters. The volume of a river is the quantity of water that it discharges, and it is measured in cubic feet per second (ft3/s).

The Amazon River, in South America, is the largest river in the world by volume.

It has an average flow rate of 7,400,000 ft3/s. That means it could fill more than 80 Olympic pools in one second. The volume of a river can vary greatly during a year, depending on the amount of rain in a season — as happens with the Nile (in Africa) — or the quantity of snow that has accumulated in the mountains.

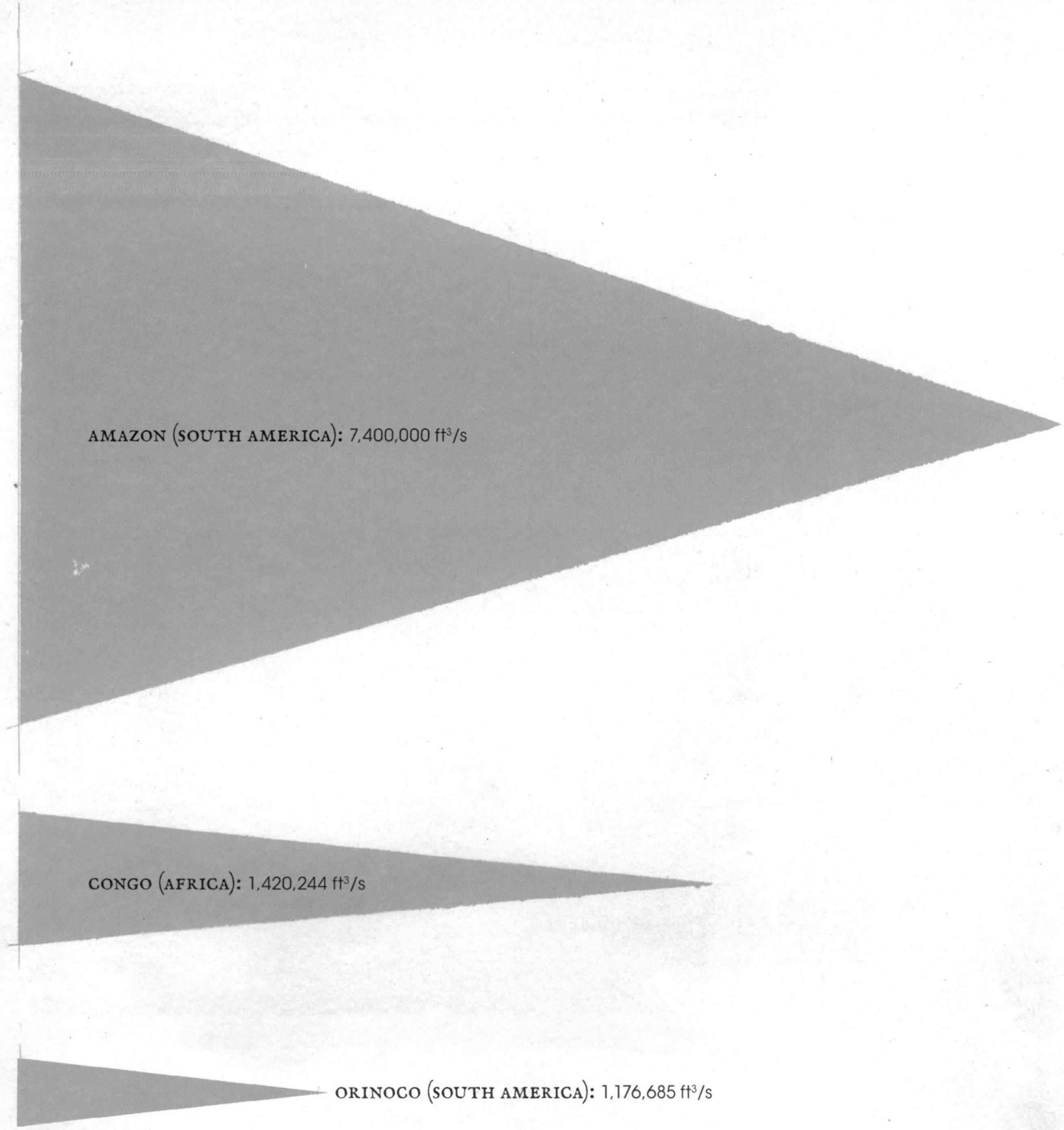

AMAZON (SOUTH AMERICA): 7,400,000 ft³/s

CONGO (AFRICA): 1,420,244 ft³/s

ORINOCO (SOUTH AMERICA): 1,176,685 ft³/s

YANGTZE (ASIA): 983,725 ft³/s

NILE (AFRICA): 98,104 ft³/s

RHINE (EUROPE): 81,224 ft³/s

NILE (AFRICA): 4,135 mi

AMAZON (SOUTH AMERICA): 3,980 mi

YANGTZE (CHINA, ASIA): 3,964 mi

YELLOW RIVER (CHINA, ASIA): 3,395 mi

PARANA (SOUTH AMERICA): 3,032 mi

CONGO (AFRICA): 2,920 mi

AMUR-HEILONG (ASIA): 2,761 mi

LENA (RUSSIA, ASIA): 2,734 mi

MEKONG (ASIA): 2,703 mi

MACKENZIE (CANADA, NORTH AMERICA): 2,641 mi

NIGER (AFRICA): 2,600 mi

YENISEI (ASIA): 2,543 mi

MISSOURI (UNITED STATES, NORTH AMERICA): 2,540 mi

MISSISSIPPI (UNITED STATES, NORTH AMERICA): 2,340 mi

OB (RUSSIA, ASIA): 2,268 mi

ZAMBEZI (AFRICA): 2,200 mi

VOLGA (EUROPE): 2,193 mi

PURUS (SOUTH AMERICA): 1,995 mi

YUKON (NORTH AMERICA): 1,980 mi

RIO GRANDE (NORTH AMERICA): 1,900 mi

SAINT LAWRENCE (NORTH AMERICA): 1,900 mi

SAO FRANCISCO (BRAZIL, S. AMERICA): 1,811 mi

BRAHMAPUTRA (ASIA): 1,790 mi

INDUS (ASIA): 1,790 mi

DANUBE (EUROPE): 1,770 mi

The *The* LENGTH *of* RIVERS

The two longest rivers on Earth
are the Nile (in Africa) and the
Amazon (in South America).

Measuring the exact length of a river is not easy, as it
is not always clear where one begins. Big rivers tend
to have tributaries (smaller rivers that flow into a main
one), which form what is called a fluvial system. The
entire fluvial system (rivers and tributaries combined)
could be counted as one unit.

The BIGGEST LAKES
in the WORLD

A lake is a mass of water that accumulates in an area with a lower altitude than the surrounding land mass. The water can come from rivers, precipitation, melting glaciers, or groundwater. Some lakes are made by humans, or animals such as beavers.

There are millions of lakes on Earth, 25 of which are larger than 2,400 square miles.

Most of the great lakes are found in the Northern hemisphere, and originated thousands of years ago as the result of glaciations. Others are the result of movement of the tectonic plates, or the action of a volcano. Almost all lakes are fresh water, but there are a few saltwater lakes, like the Caspian Sea, which is the largest in the world (and despite its name, is a lake).

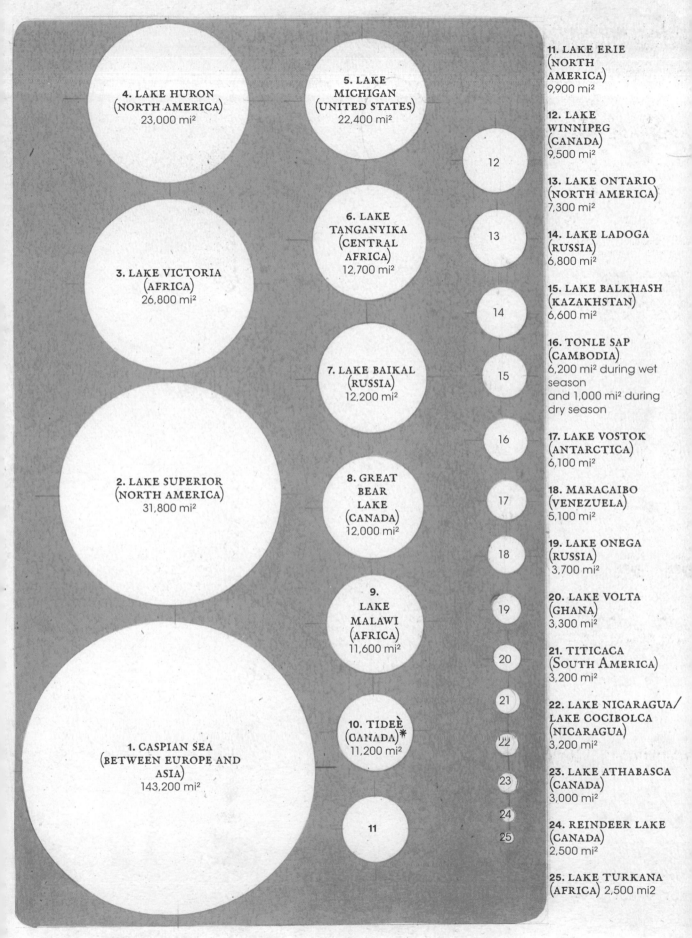

4. LAKE HURON (NORTH AMERICA) 23,000 mi²

5. LAKE MICHIGAN (UNITED STATES) 22,400 mi²

3. LAKE VICTORIA (AFRICA) 26,800 mi²

6. LAKE TANGANYIKA (CENTRAL AFRICA) 12,700 mi²

7. LAKE BAIKAL (RUSSIA) 12,200 mi²

2. LAKE SUPERIOR (NORTH AMERICA) 31,800 mi²

8. GREAT BEAR LAKE (CANADA) 12,000 mi²

9. LAKE MALAWI (AFRICA) 11,600 mi²

1. CASPIAN SEA (BETWEEN EUROPE AND ASIA) 143,200 mi²

10. TIDEÈ (CANADA)* 11,200 mi²

11

12

13

14

15

16

17

18

19

20

21

22

23

24

25

11. LAKE ERIE (NORTH AMERICA) 9,900 mi²

12. LAKE WINNIPEG (CANADA) 9,500 mi²

13. LAKE ONTARIO (NORTH AMERICA) 7,300 mi²

14. LAKE LADOGA (RUSSIA) 6,800 mi²

15. LAKE BALKHASH (KAZAKHSTAN) 6,600 mi²

16. TONLE SAP (CAMBODIA) 6,200 mi² during wet season and 1,000 mi² during dry season

17. LAKE VOSTOK (ANTARCTICA) 6,100 mi²

18. MARACAIBO (VENEZUELA) 5,100 mi²

19. LAKE ONEGA (RUSSIA) 3,700 mi²

20. LAKE VOLTA (GHANA) 3,300 mi²

21. TITICACA (SOUTH AMERICA) 3,200 mi²

22. LAKE NICARAGUA/ LAKE COCIBOLCA (NICARAGUA) 3,200 mi²

23. LAKE ATHABASCA (CANADA) 3,000 mi²

24. REINDEER LAKE (CANADA) 2,500 mi²

25. LAKE TURKANA (AFRICA) 2,500 mi2

*OR TINDE'E, TU NEDHÉ, OR TUCHO

The TIDES

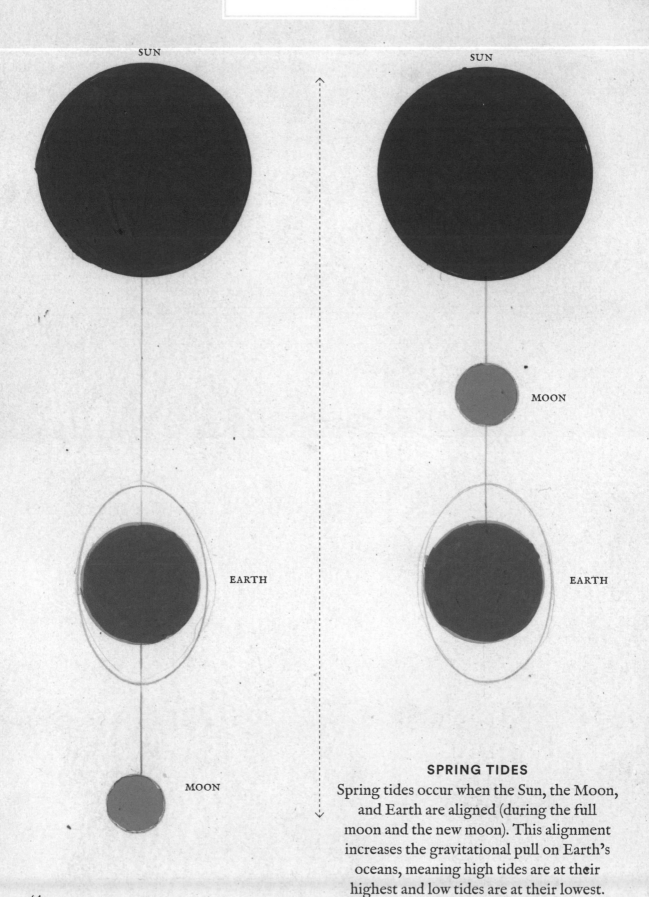

SUN

SUN

MOON

EARTH

EARTH

MOON

SPRING TIDES
Spring tides occur when the Sun, the Moon, and Earth are aligned (during the full moon and the new moon). This alignment increases the gravitational pull on Earth's oceans, meaning high tides are at their highest and low tides are at their lowest.

Twice a day, the level of water
in the oceans rises several feet
and then subsides again. This
phenomenon is called the tides.

It is caused by the Moon's gravitational pull on our planet,
as well as the Sun's (at a lower intensity), which draws the
water in the oceans in various directions, depending on the
positioning of the Moon, Sun, and Earth.

When these two celestial bodies are aligned, the force of
attraction rises and produces more extreme tides — high
tides are higher than average, and low tides are lower.

On the other hand, when the Moon is in quadrature,
or 90 degrees away from the Sun, its gravitational
forces are counteracted by the Sun — high tides are
lower than average and low tides are higher.

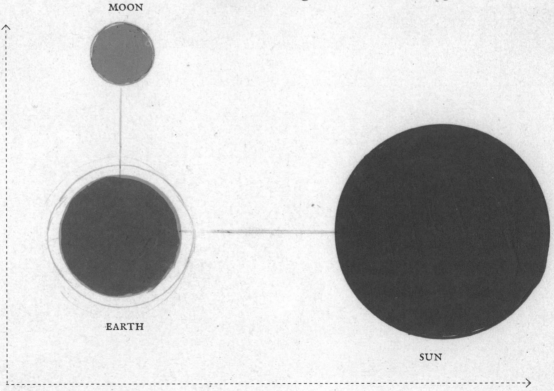

MOON

EARTH

SUN

NEAP TIDES

Neap tides occur when the Moon is in
quadrature with the Sun. When this occurs,
the Moon and Sun's gravitational forces
counteract each other, meaning the oceans'
high and low tides are less extreme.

Chapter V

CLIMATE

On Earth there are places where it rarely rains, such as deserts, and other places where it rains a lot, such as tropical rain forests. There are regions where it is always hot, and others where the temperature is permanently below zero degrees Fahrenheit.

The climate of a place depends above all on its latitude (the point on the planet where it is located, measured by distance from Earth's equator) and its altitude (or elevation) above sea level.

It also depends on land usage, and how far the land is from an ocean or other body of water. All of these factors determine the temperature, humidity, amount of rain, and even the winds, which together make up the climate of a place.

Climatic conditions determine the kinds of plants and animals that live somewhere and that together form a system of ideal equilibrium.

But pollution and the accumulation of gases in the atmosphere are increasingly causing Earth's surface to heat up, and the equilibrium between climates and plants and animals is being unsettled as the global climate of our planet changes. We are already seeing the negative effects of global climate change, such as extreme weather and melting ice caps (resulting in rising sea levels). Science experts warn that if we don't find a solution, the future consequences could be very serious.

The *The* CLIMATE ZONES

The equator is the imaginary line that divides our earthly sphere into two halves: the Northern hemisphere and the Southern hemisphere.

The equator is situated at 0 degrees of latitude. It's also the place where the Sun's rays hit most directly all year round, and for this reason, it's very hot. As we get farther away from the equator, the rays of the Sun hit Earth in a more inclined way, and thus the temperature goes down. According to latitudes, our planet can be divided into three great climate zones:

the tropical zone, with high temperatures all year long; the temperate zone, where summers are hot and winters are cold; and the polar zone, where it is always cold.

But because other factors like rainfall and topography influence climate, we may find different climates within each zone. In the tropical zone, for instance, there are places with a tropical climate that are very humid, with lots of rainfall. But there are other places in the same zone that have a desert climate, where it is very dry and there is almost no rain.

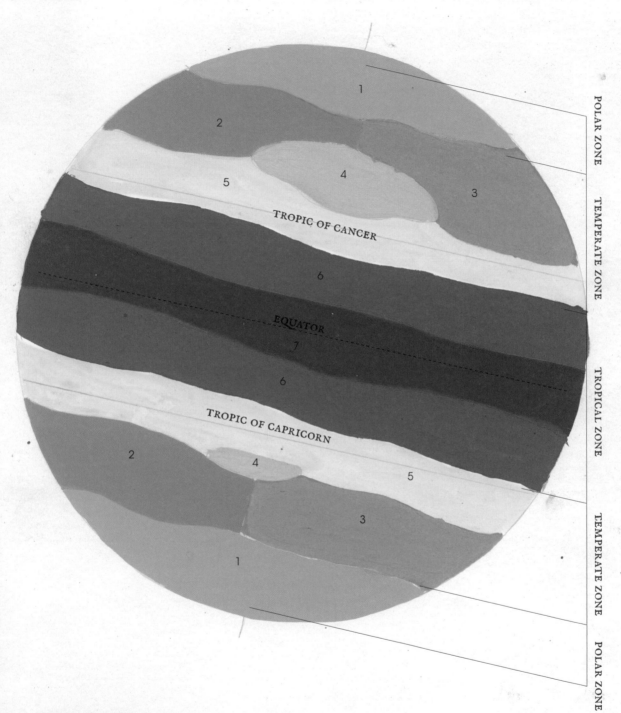

POLAR ZONE

TEMPERATE ZONE

TROPICAL ZONE

TEMPERATE ZONE

POLAR ZONE

TROPIC OF CANCER

EQUATOR

TROPIC OF CAPRICORN

SOME CLIMATE CATEGORIES:

1. POLAR CLIMATE
2. OCEANIC CLIMATE
3. CONTINENTAL CLIMATE
4. MEDITERRANEAN CLIMATE
5. DESERT CLIMATE
6. MILD CLIMATE
7. EQUATORIAL CLIMATE

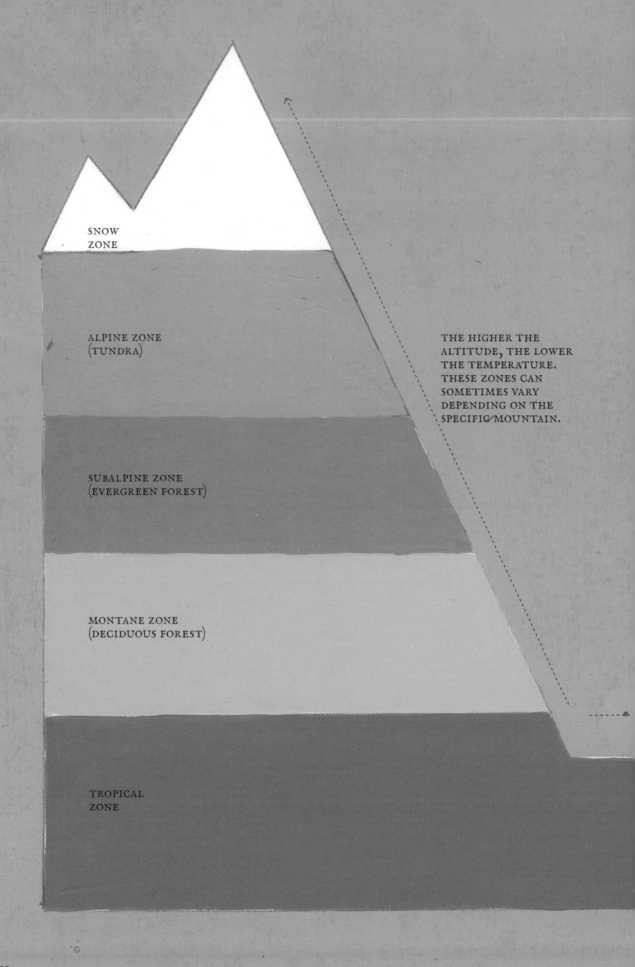

SNOW
ZONE

ALPINE ZONE
(TUNDRA)

SUBALPINE ZONE
(EVERGREEN FOREST)

MONTANE ZONE
(DECIDUOUS FOREST)

TROPICAL
ZONE

THE HIGHER THE
ALTITUDE, THE LOWER
THE TEMPERATURE.
THESE ZONES CAN
SOMETIMES VARY
DEPENDING ON THE
SPECIFIC MOUNTAIN.

BIOMES

The climate, vegetation, and animals of a specific place form a system that is called a biome.

Biomes depend on their latitude (because climates change depending on the distance of a place from the equator) but also on their altitude (as climatic conditions vary depending on how elevated they are from sea level). As a result, when you climb up a mountain, the temperature gets lower and the vegetation changes.

At the top of the highest mountains, we find conditions that are like those in the polar regions of the planet.

THE HIGHER THE LATITUDE, THE LOWER THE TEMPERATURE, GENERALLY.

DESERTS

The desert, one of the main biomes
of Earth, is an arid and dry place,
where it almost never rains.

Only a few species of very special plants and
animals can survive there. Although we often think
of sand dunes when we imagine the desert, like the
Sahara in Africa, there are rocky deserts that have
severely cold winters, like the Gobi in Asia. Large
parts of the Antarctic and Arctic are deserts too,
called polar deserts.

In the desert, temperatures are
extreme. In the Sahara, for instance,
temperatures reach 100 degrees
Fahrenheit during the day and drop to
25 degrees Fahrenheit at night.

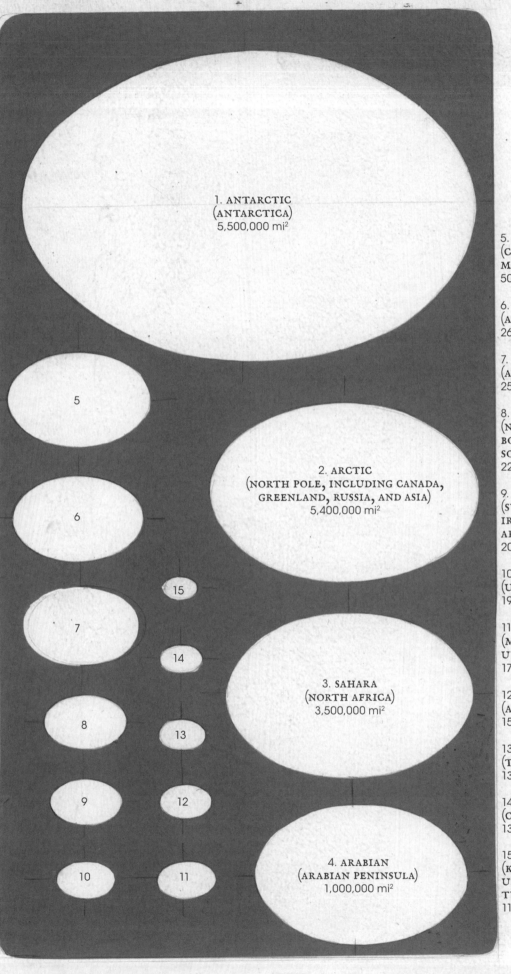

1. ANTARCTIC
(ANTARCTICA)
5,500,000 mi²

5

6

7

8

9

10

15

14

13

12

11

2. ARCTIC
(NORTH POLE, INCLUDING CANADA,
GREENLAND, RUSSIA, AND ASIA)
5,400,000 mi²

3. SAHARA
(NORTH AFRICA)
3,500,000 mi²

4. ARABIAN
(ARABIAN PENINSULA)
1,000,000 mi²

5. GOBI
(CHINA AND
MONGOLIA)
500,000 mi²

6. PATAGONIAN
(ARGENTINA)
260,000 mi²

7. GREAT VICTORIA
(AUSTRALIA)
250,000 mi²

8. KALAHARI
(NAMIBIA,
BOTSWANA, AND
SOUTH AFRICA)
220,000 mi²

9. SYRIAN
(SYRIA, JORDAN,
IRAQ, AND SAUDI
ARABIA)
200,000 mi²

10. GREAT BASIN
(UNITED STATES)
190,000 mi²

11. CHIHUAHUAN
(MEXICO AND THE
UNITED STATES)
175,000 mi²

12. GREAT SANDY
(AUSTRALIA)
150,000 mi²

13. KARAKUM
(TURKMENISTAN)
135,000 mi²

14. TAKLAMAKAN
(CHINA)
130,000 mi²

15. KYZYLKUM
(KAZAKHSTAN,
UZBEKISTAN,
TURKMENISTAN)
116,000 mi²

HURRICANES

Hurricanes are storms that produce
high-speed, rotating winds.

They originate in warm waters, typically found in tropical
zones. Warm ocean water evaporates and rises into the lower
atmosphere. When warm winds collide, they move upward,
dragging this humid water vapor up as well, which forms
clouds. The warm ocean water continues to evaporate,
providing energy for the storm to build. Winds and Earth's
rotation cause the storm to spin quickly.

Hurricanes are often accompanied by heavy
rain and can cause enormous waves in the
ocean, as well as flooding.

There are five categories of hurricanes, based on
their wind speed. Their capacity for destruction
becomes greater as the wind speed increases.

CATEGORY 5
WINDS OF MORE
THAN 157 mph

CATEGORY 4
FROM 130 TO 156 mph

CATEGORY 3
FROM 111 TO 129 mph

CATEGORY 2
FROM 96 TO 110 mph

CATEGORY 1
FROM 74 TO
95 mph

RAIN

When water evaporates from the oceans and rises into
the atmosphere, it forms clouds. Because temperatures
get colder in higher parts of the atmosphere, when
the water reaches these colder zones, it condenses
and falls to the surface of Earth in the form of
precipitation, such as rain, sleet, or snow.

Rain is vital for the development of life.
It waters fields and woods, fills the rivers,
and removes dust particles from the air.

However, it is distributed very unequally over
the surface of the planet. The rainiest places
on Earth are near the equator, where it rains
almost every day during several months. And
there are also zones, like deserts, where it
rains only sparingly.

PRECIPITATION (IN MILLIMETERS PER YEAR)
Rain is measured in millimeters (mm). Each millimeter is the equivalent of a cubic liter of water per each square meter of space.

PAPUA NEW GUINEA: 3,142
INDONESIA: 2,702
PHILIPPINES: 2,348
MALDIVES: 1,972
VIETNAM: 1,821
BRAZIL: 1,761
NEW ZEALAND: 1,732
THAILAND: 1,622
CHILE: 1,522
NORWAY: 1,414
URUGUAY: 1,300
UNITED KINGDOM: 1,220
INDIA: 1,083
ETHIOPIA: 848
UNITED STATES: 715
SENEGAL: 686
CHINA: 645
ARGENTINA: 591
UKRAINE: 565
SOUTH AFRICA: 495
MOROCCO: 346
SUDAN: 250
IRAN: 228
MAURITANIA: 92
EGYPT: 18

COLOMBIA: 3,240
COSTA RICA: 2,926
SIERRA LEONE: 2,526
JAMAICA: 2,051
ICELAND: 1,940
EL SALVADOR: 1,784
PERU: 1,738
JAPAN: 1,668
CAMEROON: 1,604
MADAGASCAR: 1,513
CUBA: 1,335
SOUTH KOREA: 1,274
IRELAND: 1,118
FRANCE: 867
MEXICO: 758
GERMANY: 700
GREECE: 652
SPAIN: 636
HUNGARY: 589
AUSTRALIA: 534
ISRAEL: 435
SOMALIA: 282
MONGOLIA: 241
KUWAIT: 121
SAUDI ARABIA: 59

SOLAR RAYS

RAYS REFLECTED BY THE ATMOSPHERE

SOLAR ENERGY ABSORBED BY THE EARTH

The absorbed solar energy causes the emission of infrared rays from Earth into the atmosphere.

A portion of the infrared rays go through the atmosphere and are lost in space.

INFRARED RAYS

Rays reflected by the greenhouse effect

EARTH

ATMOSPHERE

GREENHOUSE GASES

ATMOSPHERE

THE GREENHOUSE EFFECT

CLIMATE CHANGE

Human activity is constantly adding
more gases to Earth's atmosphere.

This alters the climate of our planet because it
multiplies the "greenhouse effect," a phenomenon
where some of the solar rays that reach Earth and
are transformed into infrared rays become trapped
by the barrier of gases in Earth's atmosphere.

These gases act like the panes of
glass in a greenhouse: they let
sunlight pass through, but then trap
heat within the greenhouse.

Without the greenhouse effect, Earth would
not be habitable because it would be too cold to
sustain life. However, for decades there has been
an excessive accumulation of gasses in the barrier,
and each year, the average temperature of the
planet rises. Greenhouse gases consist of water
vapor, carbon dioxide, methane, and other gases.
The most abundant greenhouse gas released by
human activity is carbon dioxide (CO_2), which
comes primarily from burning fossil fuels.

GLOBAL WARMING

In the last few decades, the temperature of Earth's surface has increased because of increased emissions of greenhouse gases into the atmosphere. And it continues to increase even more rapidly.

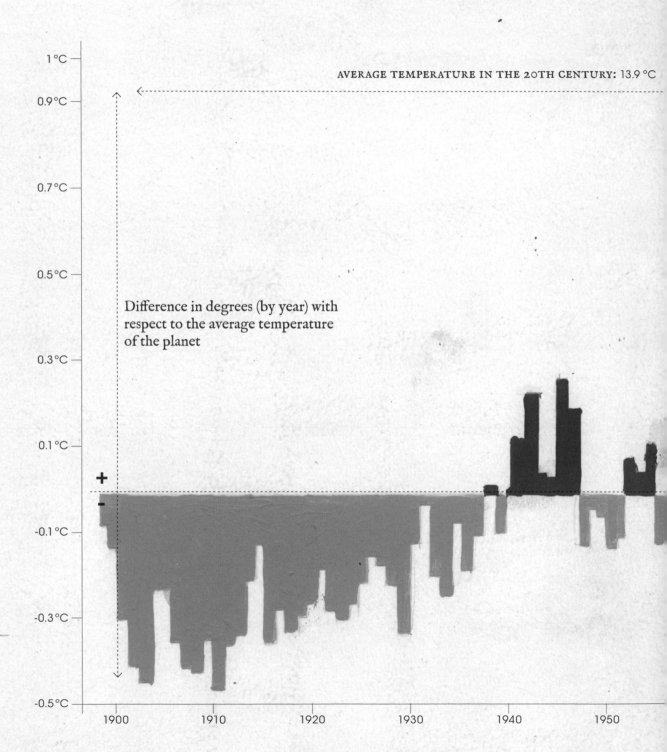

AVERAGE TEMPERATURE IN THE 20TH CENTURY: 13.9 °C

Difference in degrees (by year) with respect to the average temperature of the planet

*TO APPROXIMATE A CELSIUS TEMPERATURE IN FAHRENHEIT, JUST DOUBLE THE °C FIGURE AND ADD 30.

Global warming causes polar ice caps to melt, which leads to a number of problems. The melting ice causes global sea levels to rise, which erodes coastlines (shrinking the amount of habitable land). Snow and ice normally cover the oceans at the Earth's poles and reflect solar energy back into the atmosphere, rather than absorbing it. But as the snow and ice melt away, the oceans absorb more solar energy, causing the ocean water to heat up.

Warmer ocean water and hotter air temperatures cause more frequent extreme weather, such as hurricanes, floods, droughts, and wildfires.

EVEN IF EVERY COUNTRY MEETS IT OBLIGATIONS UNDER THE PARIS AGREEMENT, GLOBAL TEMPERATURES WILL STILL HAVE RISEN AROUND 3°C BY THE END OF THIS CENTURY (AROUND 5.4°F). WITHOUT MEANINGFUL ACTION, THIS NUMBER COULD BE AS HIGH AS 4.4°C (NEARLY 8°F).

The average temperature of the planet (during the month of July, in the 20th and 21st centuries)

1970　1980　1990　2000　2010　2020

GREENHOUSE GAS EMISSIONS

Human activity is responsible
for the production of harmful
greenhouse gases, such as carbon
dioxide and methane. The industries
that generate the most greenhouse
gases are electricity and energy
production, factories, agriculture and
deforestation, and transportation.

China is responsible for more than
a quarter of all carbon dioxide
emissions worldwide, and the United
States is next, contributing about 15%
of carbon dioxide emissions. But the
effects are felt by the entire globe.

International organizations warn
that we must arrive at worldwide
agreements to reduce these
emissions if we want to avoid even
greater global warming.

TOTAL EMISSIONS

of CO$_2$ by country in 2018
(in millions of tons)

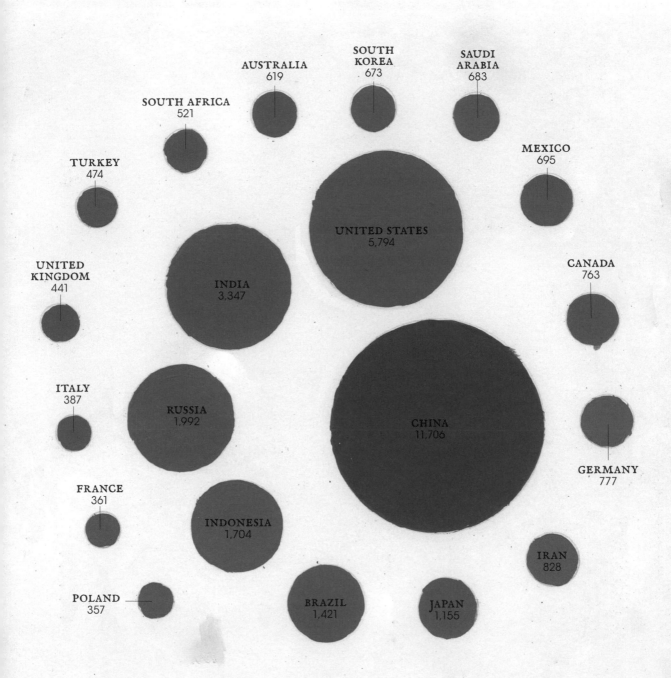

GLOSSARY

Altitude - the height of an object above ground level

Atlas - a book of maps

Area - the amount of space a flat surface takes up

Asteroid - rocks floating around in space - they vary in size greatly and can be as big as hundreds of miles across

Celestial - relating to the sky, or outer space

Comet - a cosmic snowball - as it flies through space, a comet lets off a tail of gas and dust, which can give off light when it is close to the sun

Condense - to change from a gas into a liquid

Conical - cone-shaped

Crevice - a narrow opening, especially in a rock or wall

Diameter - a straight line passing from side to side through the center of an object or shape, especially a circle or sphere

Elliptical - oval-shaped

Emission - the production and release of something, especially gas or radiation

Equilibrium - a state of balance

Evaporate - to turn from liquid to gas

Fluid - able to flow easily like a liquid or gas

Fossil fuels - a natural fuel such as coal or gas, formed in the past from the remains of living organisms

Gas - a kind of matter without a definite volume or shape

Gravity - a force that attracts two objects toward each other

Glaciation - the process of being covered by glaciers or ice sheets.

Infrared rays - a form of light that humans cannot see but can detect as heat. These waves are just a little longer than the wavelengths of red light humans can see.

Liquid - a kind of matter with a definite volume but whose shape adapts to the shape of the container it's in

Matter - the physical substance that everything is made of

Molten - turned into liquid by heat

Obscure - to keep from being seen

Particle - a tiny amount or small piece of something

Polygon - a flat shape

Satellite - an object that orbits around another object, like the moon

Solid - a kind of matter with a definite volume and shape

Topography - the arrangement of the physical features of an area. This includes natural features like mountains and lakes or man-made features like roads.

Ultraviolet - a form of light that humans cannot see but can detect as heat. These waves are just a little shorter than the wavelengths of violet light humans can see.

Volume - the amount of space something takes up

Water vapor - water when it takes the form of a gas

SOURCES

I. THE UNIVERSE

NASA Space Place
spaceplace.nasa.gov

NASA Exoplanet Exploration
exoplanets.nasa.gov

NASA Science: Solar System Exploration
solarsystem.nasa.gov

Science X
Phys.org

Australia Telescope National Facility
atnf.csiro.au

Sky & Telescope
skyandtelescope.org

Astronomy Now
astronomynow.com

II. THE PLANET EARTH

National Geographic
nationalgeographic.org

UCAR Center for Science Education
scied.ucar.edu

National Weather Service
weather.gov

U.S. Geological Survey
usgs.gov

The Alaska Earthquake Center
earthquake.alaska.edu

World Population Review
worldpopulationreview.com/continents

WorldAtlas
worldatlas.com

UN System-wide Earthwatch
islands.unep.ch/tiarea

III. TOPOGRAPHY

National Ocean and Atmospheric
Administration
oceanservice.noaa.gov

The Geological Society
geolsoc.org.uk

Geoscience Data Journal
rmets.onlinelibrary.wiley.com/
journal/20496060

National Geographic
nationalgeographic.org

Woods Hole Oceanographic Institution
whoi.edu

U.S. Geological Survey
usgs.gov

Project Base8000
projectbase8000.com

Smithsonian Institution, National Museum of
Natural History, Global Volcanism Program
volcano.si.edu

San Diego State University, College of
Sciences
sci.sdsu.edu/how_volcanoes_work/
Controls.html

IV. WATER

National Ocean and Atmospheric
Administration
oceanservice.noaa.gov

U.S. Geological Survey
usgs.gov

NOAA Climate.gov
climate.gov

NOAA National Centers for Environmental
Information
ngdc.noaa.gov

Food and Agriculture Organization of the
United Nations
fao.org/3/u8480e/U8480E3h.jpg

Geography Realm
geographyrealm.com

MDPI
mdpi.com/about/journals

National Park Service
nps.gov

WorldAtlas
worldatlas.com

NASA Earth Observatory
earthobservatory.nasa.gov

NOAA Center for Operational
Oceanographic Products and Services
tidesandcurrents.noaa.gov

V. CLIMATE

National Geographic
nationalgeographic.org

NASA Global Climate Change
climate.nasa.gov/effects

NOAA SciJinks
scijinks.gov/climate-zones

NOAA Ocean Exploration
oceanexplorer.noaa.gov/facts/
hurricanes.html

National Weather Service
weather.gov

NOAA Climate.gov
climate.gov

The World Bank
data.worldbank.org/indicator/
AG.LND.PRCP.M?end=2017&star
t=2017&view=bar

Natural Resources Defense Council
nrdc.org

U.S. Environmental Protection Agency
epa.gov

U.S. Climate Resistance Toolkit
toolkit.climate.gov

National Snow & Ice Data Center
nsidc.org

Union of Concerned Scientists
ucsusa.org

Climate Watch
climatewatchdata.org/ghg-
*emissions?end_year=2018&start_*
year=1990

The artist

REGINA GIMÉNEZ

As a child, Regina scanned through old atlases, captivated by their beautiful pictures and maps, voraciously looking for facts about Earth. In the past few years, as an acclaimed artist in her home city of Barcelona, she has returned to these images to transform them into magnificent prints, brimming with color.

In *Geo-Graphics*, Regina combines, repeats, and superimposes shapes and images, playing with colors and textures to transport us into a magical universe, replete with references to our grandparents' antique books and with updated facts and information.

SOME NOTES ON THIS BOOK'S PRODUCTION

The art for the jacket, case, and interiors was created by Regina Giménez.
The text and display were set by Semadar Megged and Irene Vázquez in
IM_Fell, a serif designed by Italian designer Igino Marini and meant to evoke
the types bequeathed to the University of Oxford by Dr. John Fell in the 17th
century — the oldest punches and matrices surviving in England. The display
was set in Circular Std-Bold, from the geometric sans-serif font family designed
by Laurenz Brunner for Lineto in 2013, a fresh take on the geometric grotesks
popular in pre-war Germany. Both text and display were chosen by the original
publisher, Zahori, to evoke the feel of old atlases. The book was printed on
FSC™-certified 160gsm Golden Sun woodfree paper and bound in China.

Production was supervised by Freesia Blizard
Book jacket, case, and interiors designed by
Feriche Black and Semadar Megged
Edited by Nick Thomas